BETWEEN THE CREEKS

Recollections of Northeast Texas

BETWEEN THE CREEKS

Recollections of Northeast Texas

By Deborah Brown & Katharine Gust

Austin THE ENCINO PRESS 1976

TO BARK & BILL

And to all those who welcomed us into their homes and helped us to understand the world between the creeks.

ACKNOWLEDGMENTS

We thank our narrators who gave so generously of their time and who accepted the intrusion of our cameras and tape recorders with patience and good humor. Unfortunately we were unable to use all the excellent material that we gathered. The text was chosen to reinforce the mood of the photographs; the quotation was not in all cases spoken by the subject of the picture.

Browntown
Mrs. Allie Baker
Clayton E. Browne
Ola Mae and Charlie Forsythe
Tommie and Clive Knight
Dezzie and Dutch Love
Olen Love
Seaby Love
Flossie and Charlie Page
Mrs. Josie Williams

Evergreen
Theodus Baker
Maria and T. C. Gamble
Dewitt Gamble
Dan Henderson
Naomi and Charlie Hill
Flora and Frank Lawson
Mrs. Mattie Logan
Loyd Logan
Mrs. McNola Peel

Sugar Hill
Bennie and Friebert Anschutz
Alvin Blalock
Gussie and Buck Blalock
Ollie Blalock
Rosalie and Tobe Cooper
J. I. Crump
Roy Gentry
Mrs. Sally Haren
Mrs. Ruby Harris
Shirley and W. D. Holt
Velver and Sam Johnson
Alice and Jewel Lum
Howard Petty
Nellie and Cliff Phillips
Rillerbelle and John Smith
Joe Smith

General
Harry Beasley
Hazel and Arthur Cameron
W. Morris Coates
Mrs. Lucille Connally
Mrs. Addie Dalby
Lucy and Clyde Dalby
Mrs. Maxine Davis
Pris and Nolan Derrick
Mrs. Ella Foster
Jo Ann and Bill Foster
David Giles
Mrs. Ollie Mae Heard
Mrs. Irma Hampden
Mrs. Izola Hughes
Mrs. Allonie Jackson
Mrs. Roberta Love
Trixie and Randy Moore
Randy G. Moore
Wilma and Joe Moore
Hattie and Earl Pirkie
Traylor Russell
Floyd Shelton
Royce Thigpen
Gena and Harold Wallace
Alec Woods

We also thank Walter and Virginia Carter, Sue Madden, Louise Ramsey and all the others on the ranch for their invaluable help; Betty Key for her guidance on the techniques of oral history; William Piltzer for his advice on photography; and Bill Wittliff for his encouragement all along the way. Finally we acknowledge our debt to Traylor Russell's book, *History of Titus County*, which filled in gaps in the history of the land between the creeks.

PLATES

19 TEXAS
JVH-899

INTRODUCTION

If you don't want no trouble, don't never drink no water out o' Sulphur River. Once you take a drink, you'll never let it alone. Makes no difference where you go, you'll always come back.

The Sulphur River winds through the switchcane bottoms of Northeast Texas "like a bowl full o' chitlins." Its muddy waters, hiding logs and water moccasins, flow past trees that cling to eroded bluffs by a few twisted roots. Unpredictable, the river can rise as much as ten feet in a night. A trickle one day, it can overflow the bottoms the next. The White Oak Creek joins the Sulphur in a maze of sloughs and bayous not far from the Arkansas and Oklahoma borders. The land between, from the fork of the rivers to Sugar Hill some twenty miles to the west, has always been known as "between the creeks."

Accustomed to the lush greens of the East Coast, we found the land between the creeks flat and drab when we first came fifteen years ago. The midday sun, harsh and brutal in the open, filters through the trees in the bottoms, lending eerie forms to fallen logs and Spanish moss. All that remains of an old homestead is a batch of bright yellow daffodils, planted decades ago by the settler's wife. Hidden under tangles of brush and honeysuckle are old grave markers with only initials to tell who lies buried there. Tales of wolves and rattlers, rides through river bottoms where even natives had been known to get lost, and rumors of moonshiners and family feuds aroused our curiosity.

Unable to find much written history about the area, we turned to the old-timers for the story. We met gracious and eloquent people who had lived near the rivers all their lives, who "knowed every tree in the bottom." What emerged from their memories was their love for an inhospitable land. Isolated from the outside world, these settlers mantained a wit and independence that have all but disappeared from the rest of the country. Education, paved roads, and television have opened up the area, but the old-timers still remember when it was uncleared and unfenced.

It was a free part of the world at that time, free. You'd start in here, ride plum to Avery horseback an' never cross a fence, never cross nothin'. Wide open.

Until the 1940s the changes of the twentieth century passed on either side of the rivers, seldom touching the lives of those between. The few roads into the area became a sea of mud when it rained, forcing the people to rely on themselves. Many women acted as midwives, since it sometimes took hours for a town doctor to cross the rivers. The "law" rarely came between the creeks, finding it difficult to penetrate both the thickets and the defenses of the people. Left to themselves, they developed their own code, based on their unwillingness "to let people run over 'em." One old-timer wistfully reflected, "You can't do nothin' now without gittin' executed. Law, law, law, law, law. So many laws you can't abide by 'em."

A small farmer, dependent on weather and the markets and equipped with the simplest of farm tools, could barely break even in a good year. Sharecroppers, who paid up to half their crop to the landowner, had a more difficult time. Although they planted peanuts, corn and other crops, this was mainly cotton country. The whole family worked in the fields, and sometimes children as young as six chopped cotton, standing in sand hot enough to raise blisters on their feet. The men also raised stock, and the bottoms were filled with half-tamed cattle, wild horses, and hogs. For additional income the settlers cut crossties and barrelheads from the timber.

In the nineteenth century the land between the creeks was covered with hardwood timber. In 1900 the Sullivan Sanford Lumber Company of Cincinnati, Ohio, bought 20,000 acres near the forks of the rivers. They built a sawmill in Naples and a railroad to bring the timber to the mill. Crossing the White Oak on a trestle bridge, the tram ran west between the creeks, past Evergreen, and ended just east of Sugar Hill. The company hauled out three loads of logs a day, until, having cut all the timber, they declared bankruptcy and closed the mill. The lumbering had changed the land completely. A thickety underbrush grew up where once the woods were so clear that "anybody could use a lariat rope could rope a rabbit." They tore up the tracks when they left, but the "ol' tram" road, then only a mud track, remained the main east-west thoroughfare for the farmers between the creeks.

Until the 1940's there were three towns on the tram, Evergreen, Sugar Hill, and Browntown. Although their development was different, they shared a common way of life. Of the three, only Sugar Hill remains.

My mother was born in Evergreen, an' when she died, she was ninety one. There was people livin' in there when she was born. They was there over a hundred years.

Shortly after the Civil War several ex-slaves settled between the creeks and soon a sizable black settlement developed. By 1900 log cabins lined the tram. Because there was little rock in the area, the settlers built their chimneys out of mud and straw, keeping a long pole nearby to push the chimney away from the house if it caught fire. Mose Price and Green Logan, for whom Evergreen was named, became two of the most successful farmers between the creeks, each having several sharecropper farmers living on their land. Others were not as fortunate. One man remembers his daddy owning 90 acres, then wanting to buy 100 more. He put the first 90 up as collateral, then "on up through the game, times got hard, an' he losed it all."

There was a church and a school in Evergreen, and Mose Price ran a store where the settlers could buy most supplies. The school, which was run by the Sugar Hill trustees, sometimes met as little as two months a year. The church was a gathering place for blacks on both sides of the White Oak, and many people remember driving miles up the tram to go to "preachin' Sunday."

The towns were segregated, but blacks and whites worked together in the bottoms, either cutting timber or helping each other with their stock. Mose Price had a "travelers' bed" where white folks stayed when they were down the tram.

Now Sugar Hill's got a bad name, but I'm gonna drop you a thought just like I've told a whole lot of 'em. A lot o' this here meanness, that Sugar Hill got the blame fer, was from somebody else who'd come in, pull these stunts, an' go back an' talk it. Everthin' fer miles aroun' kinda looks down on Sugar Hill, but this is like anywhere else, some good people an' some bad ones.

Most people think the name of Sugar Hill came from the tons of sugar hauled in to the moonshiners, but the old-timers disagree. According to one version, the town was named after Pad Harris's wife Sug. Another claims it was because the girls were "sweet as sugar." On one thing all agree. Although the town is officially known as Wilkinson, nobody ever calls it that.

To outsiders, Sugar Hill is still known as a clannish community, famous for moonshine and violence. Most of the people in Sugar Hill are related and this, together with the isolation, fostered an intense loyalty to each other and a distrust of strangers. Some who moved into the town met a hostile reception, but others did not, and certainly those living there could count on strong support from their neighbors.

The men of Sugar Hill raised hundreds of wild horses in the bottoms. Pad Harris, one of the oldest settlers, is remembered as a "rip-snortin' kind of a feller," who at one time had 500 head running loose in the woods. The young men rode with him, glad for an escape from the monotonous work in the cotton fields.

The first moonshine was made between the creeks around the First World War. Some of the old-timers had learned the trade in the "old states" and found willing apprentices among the young men of Sugar Hill. Cliff Phillips remembers sitting on his horse one morning and seeing "smoke comin' up over here, an' one comin' up over yonder. Set right there an' counted seven stills a-runnin'. Right from that spot." The canebrakes in the bottoms hid the stills so well that it was nearly impossible for the revenuers to find them. Since the moonshiners knew the woods far better than the revenuers did, the law had to rely on rivalry between manufacturers. Often, when the price fell, one of them would "turn you in, kinda make it scarce, make the price go up." During Prohibition bootleggers came from as far as El Paso to buy whisky, and, in the Depression, what had been a sideline became an economic necessity. The boll weevil had ruined cotton farming, and horse and hog prices were low. There are countless tales of people walking miles to work for 50¢ a day. The market for whisky continued strong and supported more than one family between the creeks.

The oil boom in Talco, ten miles west of Sugar Hill, brought a new era of violence to the area. Drawn to Sugar Hill by the moonshine, the oil workers often came into bloody conflict with the residents. Some oil was found in Sugar Hill itself, but it had little effect on the local population. The oil companies had bought the leases at very low prices and brought in their own crews to work the rigs.

We had a good time over there, we had a hard time. There wasn't no easy time about it. I guess we'd still be in Browntown, but Pewitt started buyin', an' that Depression. People commenced to leavin' out o' there, the school broke up, an' we all had to git out. It was just home to us, all our kids was raised there.

In 1917 the Sullivan Sanford Lumber Company sold their land to Clayton D. Browne, a real estate developer from Dallas, who planned to start a community. He divided the land into 80- to 100-acre parcels and had twelve box-houses built along the tram. For several families who had been sharecroppers, this was a chance to fulfill their dream to own land of their own. They were the last pioneers, willing to go out in rough country to establish their settlements. Although the farms were small, they could use all 20,000 acres to run their stock and could cut the timber for cash. They had to clear land and make a crop before they could pay their debt, but financial arrangements with Browne were loose. Some paid for their land; others just lived on it.

The Pages, the Loves, and the Van Hooses were among the first families to move in, and by 1921 there were enough children in Browntown to have a school. In 1922 the settlers floated a bond and built a two-teacher, white clapboard school building.

The Depression ruined any hopes the settlers had for paying off their debts, and some just turned their deeds back to Browne. In 1932 Browne, who was in some financial difficulty himself, sold the land to Dad Joiner. Joiner had discovered the East Texas Oil Field and was able to employ his reputation as a successful wildcatter to sell oil leases on the land all over the nation. The few wells that he dug came in dry and, as he had no other plans to develop the land, the people continued to live there as before.

When you quit farmin' an' let one or two ranch hands run a thousand acres, you soon lose your settlement. Takes five or six or eight to make a big cotton crop, peanuts, an' corn, but when you're puttin' it into cows, they move away. Now we ain't got no kids, no school, no land.

In 1942 this way of life came to an abrupt end. Paul Pewitt bought the land from Joiner and began to fence and clear the land. His plan to develop a cattle ranch brought him into direct conflict with the old-timers, whose survival depended on the open range. They also resented what they thought to be the ranch manager's high-handed way of dealing with them. Pewitt and his men became angry when miles of fence were cut, barns were burned, and stock was slaughtered. While only a few resorted to this violence, all were blamed. Some tried to live on the land that remained, but most bought land across the creeks and moved away. Dutch Love was one of the few who refused to sell and his uncleared tract of land sits in the middle of the ranch, a last reminder of Browntown.

Pewitt continued development, buying more land and consolidating it into a modern operation. A reserved man, he gave generously to the community, among other things building the local high school. In 1962 he sold the land to Broseco, Inc. which has continued the development.

Evergreen and Sugar Hill were also losing their populations. As the original settlers in Evergreen died, their children worked the land themselves, forcing the sharecroppers to move on. The young people moved out to find better jobs or to be nearer to schools and medical care. Finally only a few of the old ones remained. McNola Peel, Mose Price's granddaughter, came to own much of the land, which she used for a cattle ranch. In 1973 she and the other remaining owners sold their land to the Broseco Ranch. All that remains of Evergreen is the cemetery.

In 1950 Sugar Hill voted a bond issue to build a modern brick school, but it was too late. The building now stands empty, a monument to the unfulfilled dream of a community. There are still two stores in Sugar Hill where people gather to trade yarns, but the larger towns attract most of the business.

Few physical reminders remain of this world that, until thirty years ago, was close to the frontier. It now lives only in the memories of the old-timers. Their stories of life between the creeks, mellowed by many tellings, evoke this spirit far better than any words of ours can do.

RED RIVER COUNTY
BOWIE COUNTY
TITUS COUNTY
MORRIS COUNTY
SUGAR HILL
EVER GREEN
BROWN TOWN
Sulphur River
Tram Road To Naples
TRAM SPUR
White Oak Creek
MILES
COUNTY LINE

BETWEEN THE CREEKS

Recollections of Northeast Texas

Down where we lived there between them creeks, that's the wonderfulest country the world has ever seen. God never made another country better than that, an' it's still a good country. It ain't spoiled yet, but it ain't nothin' like what it used to be. There won't never no other place in the world be home with me.

COLA

We come seventy four year ago, 1900. Come up from Oklahoma—Creek Nation 'twas then. Father couldn't own no land up there, so he come off down here in the summer, found this place an' bought it. We moved down here that winter, come through in a covered wagon. We was sixteen days on the road, snow an' rain an' freezin'. You might've heard o' the coldest Friday night on record—we was out on the road that night. Lord, it was ice a foot thick.

Put this house up fore I was married. Put it up in the summer o' 1909, then I married in the fall. Built the house, moved in it, an' raised my family here. It's stood up mighty well to be just a boxed house.

I was raised on the road. My grandad had a minstrel show, just a family show. We come here to Sugar Hill in 1918 durin' the war, an' never did leave. After we stopped here awhile, why we stalled our horses, an' Grandaddy went to farmin'.

It taken me a long time to git used to farmin'. Buck used to call me a hoot owl when we married, cause I wasn't used to goin' to bed early. But I was twenty-two or twenty-three when I got married an' I learnt to farm an' milk a cow just like anybody. I said I could learn anything anybody else could.

I have an aunt, she's a wonderful housekeeper. I said to her, "When you die, they're gonna say, 'That's fer sure a nice housekeeper, an' that's all there is to it.' When I die, they're gonna say, 'Gussie was a nasty ol' housekeeper, but she sure had fun!' "

One reason I kep' that land as long as I did, it was in the family over a hundred years. My mother, she tol' me she plowed an' chopped cotton many a night by moonlight. Anybody work that hard to git hold o' somethin', an' then the children just run through it, it's a shame. I think, after all, they really did do well to come up like they did. They settled down in woods, in a thicket, an' they got out there an' cut logs an' built a little log hut with a dirt floor. I've seen 'em git dirt out of a flat, pat it, an' put grass in it, an' make them dirt chimneys. Just live offa nothin', 'cause they didn't have no money.

Clayton D. Browne, he bought him a right smart piece o' land there between them creeks an' was gonna colonize it. We lived just across the creek, an' there wasn't nothin' to keep us from knowin' that he had bought it. So we taken a notion to come over there an' settle it up; that's when we bought our land. Others kep' a comin'. Some of 'em stayed a good long while, but then Pewitt commenced a buyin', an' people commenced a leavin'. Dutch an' Dezzie, they're the only ones didn't sell out.

Below Sugar Hill, down that ol' tram, it was all in woods; there wasn't a stick o' timber cut. There was a little settlement called Evergreen, an' there was Browntown. It was all woods cept them patches they'd cleared. Wasn't nothin' below 'em til you got down twenty mile. I've seen Sulphur Bottom down there where you could see just as far as your eyes would let you see down through the woods; just nothin' but virgin timber.

We all lived there on that ol' tram, an' whenever it was rainin', why that road would git so bad. We didn't have no cars, we had to go in wagons. They'd crosslaid the road from where we lived with brush an' logs an' things like that, an' it was just a jump, jump, jump.

Browne got in contact with me, wanted to know if I'd build him some houses, an' I told him, ''Yeah.'' I hired my father an' my nephew an' we built twelve of 'em, fer a hundred dollars apiece–three box rooms, a veranda, an' a flue fer a hundred dollars. We was buildin' one a week.

I don't know how people used to live. They didn't have no screens an' the mosquiters was bad. They was what they called malarial skeeters, an' people would chill, chill, chill. They'd build those smokes in the house. I've seen lotsa floors had a hole out in the hall where the smoke bucket had burnt it. Them smokes'd die down, an' the skeeters'd just eat you up. An' sandflies, they'd just git under the covers with you, that's all there was to it. You couldn't cover up with a sheet to keep 'em off.

There was a house, ever'time anybody'd move out, there'd be somebody come through an' move in. They just named it Catch-all—it'd catch ever'thin' that come along.

We got to Browntown in the fall o' the year, an' we set in to clearin'; had to git us in a crop, you know. A few cows, a few stock, an' a crop was the only way we had to make a livin'. It was raw land, just stumpy all over. Only way o' gettin' shed o' them stumps was to take a chopax, cut 'em down, an' burn 'em. Course we couldn't cut down the big stuff. First year we didn't make too much, but the second year we made good crops. Course one feller lived here, the other there; we never did git no open space between us.

Used to, we'd go to Page Lake an' do our washin'. Bill an' Charlie would git up an' go squirrel huntin', an' I'd hitch up the wagon and git my babies, go down an' git Ada an' her bunch, an' then we would go to the river. Ada, she nearly always carried some fryers to kill, case they didn't git no squirrel. Course, them chickens'd crow goin' down there, an' she'd say, "All right, cock, you're crowin' your last time." But we'd usually git down there, an' they'd have squirrel, an' Ada'd take her chickens back home. We'd wash an' spread our clothes on the bushes to dry. Then we'd cook an' have dinner an' set around an' talk til the clothes got dry. If we had fish, we'd put 'em in the wash pot, an' then we'd load up, an' home we'd go.

After we done got up an' married an' had children, after we got over between the creeks, we had to have some kind of amusement. We'd have a gang over fer awhile, an' we'd rip an' cut up the biggest part o' the night. When we got music, we'd have a square dance. At play parties, stead of us dancin' after music, we sang. We didn't join up an' swing different things, but it was all the same thing. A lotta church members didn't agree with you dancin' with the music, but play parties was alright. I never could see no difference. I don't think, if anybody's gonna do no worse than them dances, no boogy-man's gonna git him anyway. I think there's a whole lot you can do worse than dancin'.

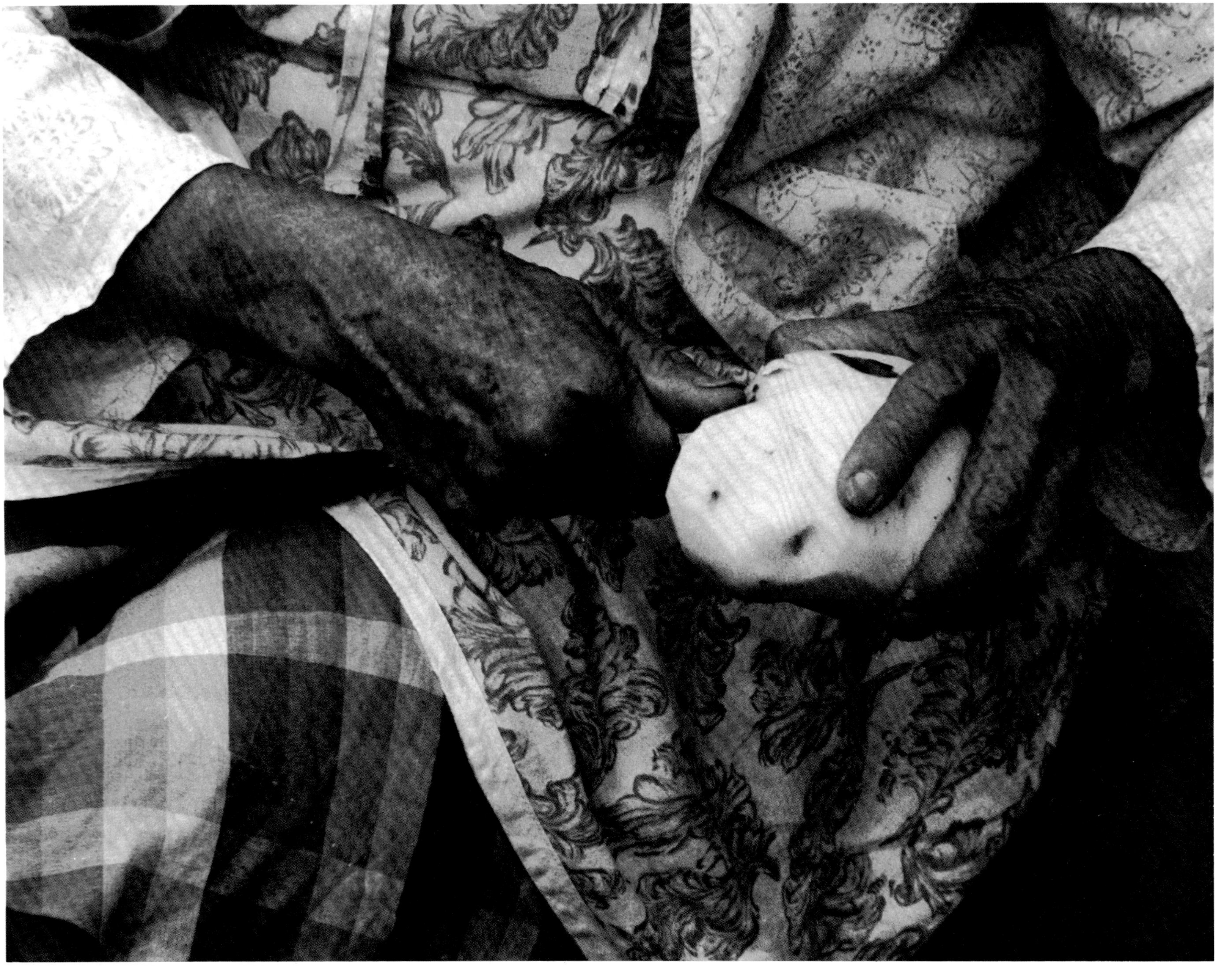

My mother never did have anythin' but just an apple box fer shelves and sack sheets fer sheets, but I'm tellin' you right now, her house was sparklin'. It was always as clean as a pin. She never did have nothin' like people nowadays have to keep house on. I said, if she had my house now, an' what I've got in it, Lord, she'd be in hog heaven. She died a few years after she got her ice-box.

We visited up the tram a few times. Oh, it was pitiful. We had to wade mud an' water from cross the White Oak slap up where Jess an' them lived. Oh, mud was that deep. We had an ol' T model car. My husband pushed that thing with ever'thin' he had from down there plum on. We got up there in it, but we had to walk an' push. That's a wonder it hadn't killed us all. It come a big freeze an' a overflow while we was up there. We had to stay a week later, had to stay, I think, two weeks, fore we could git back cross the White Oak. I tol' him then, I said, "Well, I'm gonna wash the mud off right here." I crawled over there, edge o' the water. I washed my hands an' my feet an' got in the car. I says, "I bid it adoo." An' I didn't come back fer a long time. Not til the roads got better.

They say the good ol' days, but they was hard times. Time didn't fly then, like it does now. I used to think a day was a week long, and a week was a month long. You can't tell me time ain't shortened. You know, the Bible speaks of shortenin' the days; the week's just gone; the year's gone before you know it.

Kids them days, even when they was grown, they was still kids. My gracious, I know me an' one o' my little girlfriends, we had a playhouse til we was about 16 years old. It was between her house an' my house, in a little bunch o' woods. We just had us a place cleaned off an' we had us some little shelves nailed on a tree. We'd go over ever' so often an' clean it an' fix it up. Whenever she'd git ready to go, she'd git out an' blow her fist, an' I'd answer, an' we'd meet over there an' play til maybe dark.

I really didn't think I could die when I was young. I didn't think nothin' would hurt me, an' it didn't til I guess I got smart.

It's a wonder we didn't git snakebit, but there never was none of us never did git snakebit. We run over that woods, huntin' bears an' things, barefooted. Didn't know what a shoe was.

We was purty mean in school. Me an' another feller made one six months o' school an' never missed a whippin'. We wore these britches up to here, an' black stockin's. He pulled 'em loose from my leg an' I pulled 'em loose from his where the blood was stickin'.

Wasn't nobody put no wood in the schoolhouse. We'd hep the teacher cut some, 'cause we didn't want to freeze. We'd hep him an' then we'd turn around an' do ever' mean trick just to aggravate him. Me an' some other boys, we went down there one evenin' after school. We got his bell, an' all the trinkets he kep' down there, an' we destroyed it all, carried 'em way down on the branch an' tore it up an' throwed it away. We went back up there an' tore up his desk; an' then we taken our pistols an' shot all the brick off, one brick at a time off the top o' the house. I don't guess we was very mean, just mischievous. We would fight—yeah, we'd fight, but we just called that playin', you know.

I was a granny doctor. I had to work with doctors, cause we didn't have no hospitals an' the nearest doctor was eight, ten mile. Sometimes these roads'd be so bad they couldn't hardly travel in a buggy. Lotsa times I'd be called fore the doctor would git there, an' he'd o.k. it. There were lots an' lots o' times women had their babies, never even had a doctor in the house.

Man lived below us, he was the kind o' man that drinks some. I didn't fear that, cause I'd got salvation, an' I wasn't afraid. I never was. They called me down there in the evenin', snow bout two foot deep on the ground. He carried me down in a wagon, an' long bout dark, she began to be in labor.

I thought, "Just me an' him!" She was walkin' around still, an' I went out to the barn, waded the snow out to the barn. I knelt down prayin', said, "Lord, this is one time I really need You. It's me callin' on You. It's me that needs You now."

Well, when I got back to the house, she had got in bed. I said, "Well, do you think it's time for the baby?" She said, "Yeah, the baby's here." So there I was, snow two foot deep, an' no doctor. I finished with the baby an' her too, an' they did just fine.

I remember when I was a little ol' bitty kid, my grampa, he taken down with pneumonia. The ol' man was about to kick the bucket, too. It was bad weather, snow all over the ground. Papa asked did he want him to go to Annelder an' git the doctor up there. Grampa said no. There was an ol' doctor lived over bout three, four miles from us, name o' Steddams. "Go over there git ol' Doc Steddams, cause I'd rather risk him than them other ones anyhow."

Well, Papa, he got on his horse an' took off. Bout two, three hours, here they come back. That ol' Doc Steddams, he was a little bitty guy. Bet he wouldn't o' weighed hundred-ten pounds. He was red-headed, just as red-headed as he could be, an' he wore women's high button shoes. It's a honest fact, that's the kind o' shoes he wore. He come in; Grampa was layin' there in the bed in the fireplace room. He come along to Grampa an' he spoke, said, "Ol' man, I'll be with you directly I git warm."

Well, he got over there by the fireplace an' stood around there a little bit, pulled his overcoat off. He went back to Grampa's bed, checked him over. He turned roun' to Mama an' he said, "You'd just as well fix both dinner an' supper fer me, 'cause I'm gonna be with you."

He went back there an' he set down on the side o' the bed. He pulled his shoes off, an' he got up an' straddled Grampa. Boy, I'm gonna tell you right now, you could hear that ol' man screamin' an' hollerin' all over the place. But in a little while I guess that pneumonia broke. Grampa, he started to coughin' an' spittin' that stuff up. That ol' doc, he sat up there with Grampa all night. He stayed the rest o' that day an' all the next night, too. Grampa, in a few days, he was up an' goin'.

In the wintertime, when we needed a doctor between the creeks, they'd hire somebody, bring 'em to White Oak; then we'd meet 'em there in a wagon. Lots o' times, when the water was up, we'd have to take a boat to git 'em across. Couldn't afford to git sick. One time, we was down at the forks o' the creeks, an' she got the measles, like to have died, too. We had to haul the doctor down there in a wagon. After that happened, I said, "Can't make her do that no more, let's git out from here." So we bought us a place an' moved up on the road.

There was a little girl, died while we lived between the creeks, an' the roads was real bad. Charlie got in a wagon an' went to Naples an' got her casket an' material to make her a dress to be buried in. Her mother wanted her buried in a dress like she ordinarily wore. He was til nine gittin' back, he was all day goin' to Naples, which wasn't too far. I set up til ten o'clock to make that dress. She was buried cross the creek at Roberts graveyard.

My daddy was a cow man, an' I stayed right at his heels. Since I've been married, I've tried my best to stay outside. First few years why, he'd wash the dishes while I caught the mules an' harnessed 'em up fer us to go bale the hay. I don't mind cookin', but as far as keepin' a house spic an' span, an' fine furniture an' things like that, why I don't want 'em, cause I just don't have time to do it, an' I don't think they're pretty if they're not kept right. I'd like my kids to have a nice home, but I don't want one. Shoot, I like to git out an' work in the garden an' see about the cows an' do the plantin', an' then go fishin' an' squirrel huntin'.

You couldn't starve people to death—squirrel, deer, beef—you couldn't starve to death in the land o' plenty, could you? Lord a mercy, we wasted enough fish, we oughta been prosecuted for it. We'd build a hangin' gate cross them sloughs when the creek would rise. Them fish'd go up there to feed, an' if you didn't git up there in time to shut the gate, by the time it fell that much, why they'd all be back in the creek. But if you git there in time an' shut the gate—one time we caught three wagon loads! We peddled 'em, an' while I was peddlin' 'em, course they'd die. We peddled it up to Cut Hand, bout fourteen mile cross the Sulphur, an' brought the rest back across the bridge, an' backed up to the river, an' throwed 'em all in to the hogs in the bottom.

Now I'm just gonna tell you a little tale. I had to work, an' I had to work hard, too, but when Sunday mornin' come, I'd git up fore daylight, take my dogs, an' I'd hit that bottom. I spent many a happy hour in that bottom, me an' some more ol' boys. We just went over there, just plannin' on havin' a good day. Good many ol' cat in there, an' the dogs'd sometimes git after a hog. We'd kill us some squirrel, maybe. Didn't have no closed season then. We'd kill squirrels whenever we got ready.

Me an' some other boys found us a boat an' was goin' down the Sulphur. Water was all over the bottom; just as high an' rough as could be. We was comin' down to a lake. It was forced water, an' I was tryin' to hold that boat. I wasn't able to handle it; that thing got advantage of me. It commenced turnin' round an' round an' just couldn't hold water. I hit a tree. Three of us went up the same tree. I think one o' those ol' boys got his feet wet, but me an' th'other one didn't. There we was, up in that tree, an' the water just a boilin'. I coulda swum out, but you know, I was playin' safe. The other ol' boy was a better swimmer than I was, an' we'd o' tackled the ocean if we'd taken the notion—but we never did take no notion. Boys had to come in a good boat, haul us out. Joe More an' them got my hat. It floated down a way an' lodged against some brush.

When I was bout thirteen years ol', used to be some awful thick switchcane in that bottom. Me an' my cousin was hog huntin', an' that cane was so thick we had to reach over an' tear it out from in front of our horse, so that we could go again. My horse stopped in that cane one day. I stood up in my stirrups, reached over, an' tore that cane away from his breast—when I raised up my head, a 30-30 Winchester was just about that close to my head. The man said, "It's a good thing I knowed that horse. Hadn't of, I would o' shot you." That'd give you a scare.

At one time, don't guess there was one house from Meadows Curve up here, back down between the creeks where you couldn't stop an' git a quart o' whiskey, whatever you wanted. All the merchants in Mt. Pleasant, Clarksville, all round, they was in it themselves, 'cause they got a little trade. You got a little money, why you spent it with them. They protected you. Revenuers come down, why they'd call an' tell you: "You better take in your washin'; it's gonna come a rain."

You'd see a still, an' then you'd want to go the other way. I had some runnin' in my own pasture. It was grown up with trees an' everythin' down there. I was there huntin' one day, an' right behind a pool, there was a still. I just walked on, didn't say anythin' about findin' it. The next day the revenuers came. The moonshiners knew I had been by, an' they just cut all my fences. Thought I'd turned 'em in. I didn't tell a word. It was all right with me, and if it wasn't all right, I wasn't goin' to say anythin' anyway.

Several years after we come to Sugar Hill, feller come by one mornin, borrowed my long handle shovel, had a couple buckets with him. I couldn't imagine what he was gonna do with them buckets, what he wanted to do with that shovel. I heared later he run a saloon, made whisky. He made it in his house, had it there in big troughs, kep' ice in the water to make it cold. He run it right there. He'd showed my brother-in-law the whole thing, all about it.

Wasn't long til another feller or two got to makin', an' it just taken on like wildfire. It was a year fore us boys here tried it. Me an' my brother Buck didn't know a thing about it, never seen a pot, nor a worm, nor nothin'. A cousin of ours, his Daddy had made it back in the old states, an' he'd tol' him how to make it. He come over, an' him an' Buck hitched up a wagon, an' went over here on White Oak to hire 'em some pots. They sent me on out in the pasture to dig a furnace. I didn't know no more bout diggin' a furnace than diggin' an oil well. So I went out there an' sat on a stump, sat there til midnight fore anybody come. Directly I heared the wagon, made the awfullest racket. I just sat there, didn't know nothin', lookin' on to see. They unloaded all that tin to cover the furnace with, taken out the thump keg, cap keg, a copper pot; that's the first one I'd ever seen. Set it out there an' we went to work. Got daylight fore we finished.

I stayed out all night that night, all day the next day, an' all night the next night. Come in Sunday mornin'. We was three days out there, cookin' them two barrels. Then a feller come through, said "Revenuers are comin; if you got anythin' you better git shed of it." Well we didn't know no better, didn't know if it was ready or not.

We got twenty gallon o' stuff out o' them barrels, an' a dog couldn't drink it. It was bitter, burn you up. Green beer, you know. But I hitched up my team, loaded it on the wagon, an' I carried the twenty gallon over to Hart's Bluff. A rancher over there wanted the whisky. Got it there, an' they paid me twenty dollars a gallon fer it, them ol' yella twenty dollar bills. I thought we was gonna git rich.

It'd bother you ever'time you'd sell some. You was afraid he'd go off an' kill someone. But my doctor tol' me I'd have to pay him; my banker tol' me wasn't nothin' left fer me to do. I owed three years in a row. We didn't have no money to pay debts with. They wouldn't loan you but enough to start a crop, then you had to do without the rest of the way. Had to make whisky. But I didn't drink, I never did. I don't drink it yet. I tol' 'em it wasn't made to drink —it was made to sell. You're crazy to drink somethin' you know'll kill you.

Talco boomed real big fer awhile, when that oil field first come in. They voted this wet in here, an' they had their honky tonks an' what have you. You talk about mean places, now it was a mean place. It was daresome to git out after dark less you had a pole or a gun with you. There was lots an' lots o' people git killed up roun' Talco. Lot of 'em git killed an' they never even knowed who they was. They'd find 'em dead somewhere an' never know who killed 'em, what happened.

One o' them laws, he was mean; he'd as soon shoot you, if you was runnin'. Shot a cousin o' mine in the leg with buckshot. Hollis come into court; he'd been shot in the leg—it'd been nearly a year. He was on crutches, just a hobblin' away, you know. He walked up to the judge, an' the judge charged him a dollar fine. We walked out o' the court, an' he says, "I got to tell you one thing. Throw these damn things away. I'm tired o' totin' 'em." He'd been haulin' them crutches around where people was, so he'd git out of it. His ol' Daddy an' his brother got sixty days in Paris jail, an' a $120.00 fine. He didn't git but a dollar.

I was a little baby, but I'm gonna tell you how it was, just as near as I can. Lady, you can judge fer yourself when I git through. Well, Squire Smith was just a young man, and so was Little Henry Jones. The Dillards had a grocery store in Red River County. It was a right smart little ways over there, too. Somebody commenced breakin' in that store. They come, you know, purty regular.

Dillards decided they'd catch 'em. They trailed 'em back this way toward Jones Crossing. They'd lay in that crossin' nights, see who'd cross. Squire Smith an' Little Henry Jones started to cross, and Dillards waylaid 'em; they just assumed it was Squire an' Little Henry that was breakin' in their store. And the shootin' fixed to take place. Squire killed one o' the Dillards and one o' the Dillards killed Little Henry Jones. They shot ol' Squire, too, shot him in the heel. The ol' feller like to have never got well, Mother said. I heared most of it time an' again; I was just a kid. They killed Little Henry Jones and Squire killed the Dillard right in the bed o' the creek, and it was at night when they done it.

It was a lot o' pretty wild times. Just people huntin' trouble. Them days an' times, back when I was a boy, people fought mostly with their fists. Now when you git into it with a man, he tries to kill you. Back then, if you heared of any killin', somebody shot 'em standin' behind a tree, bushwhacked. An' they had not much of a way of findin' out who done it. Just shoot a man, walk out through them woods, an' go on about your business. They'd hardly ever kill a man over just a fight. Maybe this feller shot somebody, one o' their friends or somethin' like that down the line, an' it just kep' on travelin'.

That convict farm down there was bout the roughest thing we had here. Catch a boy, don't matter what he's doin', take him out, an' work him on that farm. Sheriff stood in with the feller that owned it. They had an' ol' log crib; they locked them balls an' chains on 'em, an' locked 'em in that shack. They was workin' 'em an' makin' a profit out of 'em, see? Finally, bunch o' people got on their horses, rode over there an' tol' 'em they'd give 'em til dark to turn all them men loose. Fore dark come, they'd turned 'em loose, too. They knowed they was fixin' to come in after 'em if they hadn't.

We're good people all through here. Didn't have no trouble with nobody. Bad man come in the country, he'd just as well not stop. If he wouldn't do the right thing, they'd go to him an' tell him. He'd better do it, too; if he wouldn't fly right, he'd just better not stop.

Ol' man Pad Harris I reckon had five-hundred head o' wild horses. Anybody come along need a horse, he had it. Sold half of 'em on credit an' never got paid for 'em. They just growed wild. They didn't cost him nothin'.

He never did hire many hands; he'd always have a bunch o' boys hangin' around. He'd feed 'em an' keep 'em all the time, an' they'd hep him. He'd furnish 'em horses to ride, an' they'd just rip around all over the country, an' ride them ol' broncs.

People handle their stock different now than they did then. Used to, we had an ol' mare runnin' right in here—she carried about a hundred head o' horses with her all the time. (She never got a lick o' salt or a bite of nothin', only in that corral.) If you wanted to pen that ol' mare, pitch the corral gates fore you left the house, come down wherever you found her, give her a boost, an' she'd go just as straight home as she could go. She'd go home an' she'd carry that whole bunch o' horses with her. All you had to do was git somebody shut the gate behind 'em.

We used to come right out o' Sulphur Bottom, bring the horses there in that corral. We'd catch one, saddle him right there, git on him, open the gate, turn him out in the woods, an' maybe come in the next day drivin' a bunch o' wild horses on him. That's the way we broke horses. I broke a lot of 'em, maybe keep 'em about a month. Get 'em broke good an' gentle—why it was no fun ridin' 'em. I'd just go down, git me another one.

They've settled up an' fenced now. When they was fencin', they got our horses an' killed 'em—sell 'em fer soap, ten dollars a head. Creeks'd git up, an' we couldn't git over there. Got too old to ride, an' the boys all left. We quit, an' I never went back. There's still a few in there someplace.

We was cuttin' logs way back there in Hogs Neck Crossin', an' I seen some horse tracks. I crawled close enough to see 'em, seen an ol' mare bout thirty year old with a young colt. There was seven head. Foreman said, "You can catch 'em if you like."

I said, "You can have 'em. I couldn't catch 'em if I wanted 'em."

We had a sled made, an ol' brown sled, was bout six foot long, an' was on runners: two by eights. We had that floored, an' ever' day we'd load that up with sorghum hay an' take it to Reddon Lake, bout a mile an' a half down the road, feed our cattle. You take that ol' sled, after you run it awhile, those runners was just as slick, so it was no trouble fer a mule to pull. It wouldn't git stuck in the mud, like somethin' with wheels.

Whenever water commenced a comin' up; why we'd push the cattle up on our own high ground. We used a blowin' horn to call 'em, cows'd come just as purty. I lost mine right between them creeks an' I never in the world could find it. I had it on the saddle horn an' a limb jerked it off an' I never did find it, never did buy me another.

This ol' black bull, we called him Pluto, he'd git you, there's no question. You couldn't pick at him—he'd been fooled with. One time, me an' another ol' boy, I never will fergit it; we went over there cross White Oak to what we call the Cancel Place, had a lot o' hay there in an ol' house. Marvin, he got him a pint an' was about half lit on the way over. He got there an' ol' Pluto, he come up pretty close to that yard, an' Marvin was out there pickin' at him: shakin' his hat, an' first one thing, an' another.

I said, "Marvin, that bull's gonna git you directly." He says, "Oh no, can't git me, I'm up here on the gallery."

Bout that time, that ol' bull reared up on the gallery, just rotten anyhow, an' shook it down. Marvin went through that house out on th'other side. That ol' bull rammed his head in that door; you could hear him bawlin' a mile.

Used to, there was a lot more switchcane in Sulphur Bottom than there is now. You'd go down there an' find a bed o' switchcane as large, say, as a house, an' taller than me. But you better not ride up too close, or git off your horse, if you see steam comin' from it. There'll be just scads o' hogs up under that patch, an' when they come out, why they come out ready to fight.

Ol' man Pad Harris, I've seen him crawl over in a pen with a wild bunch o' hogs, just as wild as they come, set right down, pull his hat off when one would run at him, throw the hat at her, an' holler, "Sooee, God damn you." (He cussed just like a sailor.) An' while she was fightin' his hat, he'd be markin' pigs. How the ol' man kept from gettin' killed, I don't know.

You take them wild hogs, they'd git to fightin' the dogs, an' the dogs'd know just what to do. The hogs'd run at them dogs an' the dogs'd just keep backin' up, runnin' an' barkin' an' backin' up. They'd keep the bunch together an' run 'em right on in an' pen 'em. Maybe two dogs workin' at the side, keep 'em from runnin' off.

Back them days, say a sow had five, six pigs, you'd sell the sow fer two dollars an' throw the pigs in. Other than cotton, that was all a person had to make a livin' out of. What really hurt us so bad, me an' my Daddy, we would have to work in the field, an' while we was workin', somebody else would harvest our hogs for us. They'd drive 'em off—we couldn't find 'em. Course the ones that really kep' hogs in the woods, they got to make a success out of it. They was in the bottom ever' day, you see, keep somebody sceered out. But whenever you had to work, an' just see about your stock on days you couldn't do nothin else, well that's what made it rough.

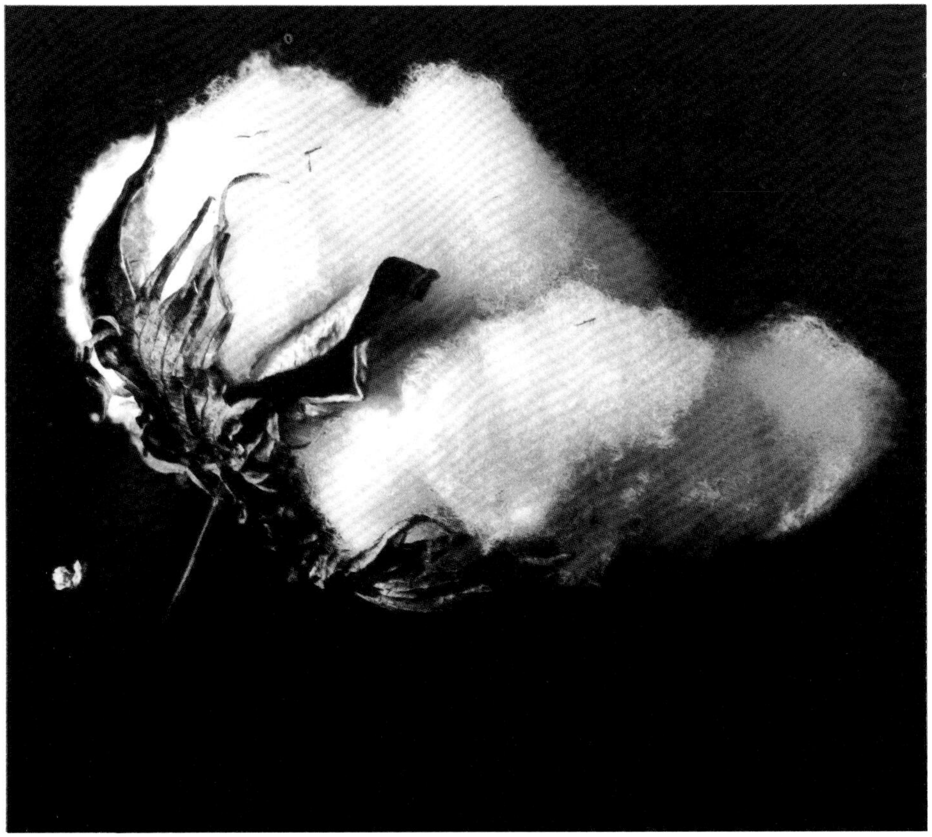

One o' my cousins, he come down here an' he tol' me, "Oh, there's people in Kansas City never seen a stalk o' cotton grow." I said, "They don't raise cotton there?" "No, nothin' but corn an' wheat an' potaters." I said, "Oh, if I can just git there." So I asked him if he'd carry me up there. He had a lot o' money, so he said he'd pay my way, an' send me back when Mama got ready to have me come home. She said, "Bout April I'll be writin' to you to come." I said OK. But deep down in my heart, I said, "I'll never come back down here an' live no more."

I stayed there seven years, but then I come on back. It was in the fall o' the year, an' I never will fergit it. They had a big cotton crop, an' that cotton was just as white as snow out there in that field. I felt sorry fer Mama, tryin' to pick it. Winter was comin' on, so I tol' her, "Mother, I left here kickin' pickin' cotton, an' I'm right back in the same place. I'm gonna git out there an' hep you pick; you can git in to the fire. An' then I'm goin' to town an' git me a job, an' I'll never pick cotton no more."

We growed cotton, that's the way I come up, an' it's a hard come up. From just a child, my lifetime right on through, cotton was all I ever knowed. An' it was hard work, too, don't you fergit it. I worked many a—no, many an' many an' many a day standin' out til the time daylight come, an' ploughed just as long as I could see.

One day I tol' him, "I'm gonna plow." He said, "You cain't plow." I said, "Other women plow—it looks easy." He said, "Well, it does look easy. I'll tell you what, there's a little piece o' land right over there, you can flat break it til you git it all broke up." I couldn't git the ol' horse to walk right, an' I got mad, an' I got to cryin', an' I said, "You give me the hardest job! Rows like you're doin' is easy." He said, "Come on, git your horse an' plow, do like I'm doin'." First thing I knowed, I was plowin right across his rows. I said, "Ain't none of it easy! I don't want to plow nohow."

AND ELIJAH TALK

We made it purty good back then cause we was on the farm. We killed enough hogs to make our meat an' our lard. We had cows fer milk an' butter, an' chickens in the yard. We made our own syrup an' we had vegetables; I've seen mama can a smoke-house full. All we had to buy was flour an' sugar. You take back then, if a man had a pea patch or roastin' ears, all of his neighbors was welcome to come in there an' pick peas. But you git in a man's pea patch now, boy, you better run.

If you made a big crop, you didn't have no money; if you made a little crop, you didn't have no money —so it was just work. All you could do when you fell behind was pull your belt up another notch. I'm tol' the clodhopper's the only person in the world can go broke ever' year, an' go back in business. You got ever'body beat when you're a clodhopper.

I can't tell you how long we used that land fer nothin'. That's the reason we didn't own none of it. We didn't have to buy it; we already had it, an' wasn't a thing said. We didn't want to pay taxes on it, when we already had it, the whole thing, you know. Just a few of us had the whole thing. That's where I tell you I made a bad mistake. We could o' bought all of it, just any part of it we wanted. We could o' bought it fer seven dollars an acre. Just as big a block or just as little a block as we wanted. Seven dollars an acre.

When Pewitt bought that land he had a difficult time. He started in to fencin' that thing an' cleanin' it up, an' those ol' boys that had lived in there all those years, they just didn't want any part of it. They cut fence just as fast as Pewitt built it. But he just kept on buildin' fences, and every once in a while one of 'em would get disgusted an' move out. Over the period of years he finally reduced it to control. The only way he made it through, was just get a bunch in that was pretty rough themselves. Never did get down to shootin' at one another, but almost got that way several times.

If they'd o' acted right, people would o' hepped 'em, took care o' their stuff til they was all finished. But they didn't care about nobody. All they wanted was the territory in here an' they set out to git it. Push people out—they'd o' just bulldozed 'em out if they could've.

Feller I know, he moved to Dallas, stayed up there ten years. He come back down here one time to go squirrel huntin'. That was after Paul Pewitt first come in. He said he knowed this place where he'd always went an' killed lots o' squirrels. Headed out that mornin', 4 o'clock, got down there in the dark. He set down, said when it come daylight, there he was, settin' middle o' the pasture, not a tree nowhere.

The best times was back thirty, forty year ago, when they had open range an' free country. Ever'-thin's cheap, people visitin'. Load up the family wagon, go stay all night, maybe a day an' night with parties, you know, three, four families in one house. Now you don't see nothin' like that. I believe it was better times than there is now. I liked 'em better, anyhow. All the settlers just about left this country, bout died out. Most o' the settlers, they gone. All them fellers used to live in here, all gone.

Type set by G & S TYPESETTERS

Printed by HART GRAPHICS

Paper supplied by LONE STAR PAPER COMPANY

Bound by CUSTOM BOOKBINDERY

Design by WILLIAM D. WITTLIFF